The House Party

The House Party

POEMS BY
CAROLINE KNOX

Caroline Knox [signature]

The University of Georgia Press
Athens

Copyright © 1984 by Caroline Knox
Published by the University of Georgia Press
Athens, Georgia 30602

All rights reserved
Set in 10 on 12 point Palatino
Printed in the United States of America

Library of Congress Cataloging in Publication Data

Knox, Caroline.
　The house party.

　I. Title.
PS3561.N686H6 1983   811'.54   83-5867
ISBN 0-8203-0676-2
ISBN 0-8203-0678-9 (pbk.)

For my family

Acknowledgments

The author and the publisher gratefully acknowledge the following publications in which poems in this volume first appeared.

The Anglican Theological Review: "Daisy or Jane?" "David"
The American Scholar: "The House Party," "Louie"
The Cream City Review: "About Calder"
A Letter Among Friends: "Grinders"
The Massachusetts Review: "Sacagawea"
The Minnesota Review: "The Painting"
Poetry: "The Cavendish Club," "The Crybaby at the Library," "The Fat Baby," "The Foamy-Necked Floater," "Green Animals," "Herbert Smith," "Hittites," "I Have Met Freddy," "Nancy Drew," "The Phoenix," "Sol Invictus," "Sports," "Walden Remaindered"
Woman Poet: The Midwest: "Do You Traipse," "Fresh Horses Should Be Waiting," "A Poem Beginning with a Line by Wyatt"

Contents

I Have Met Freddy 1
Rachel and Wally 3
The Cavendish Club 4
Sol Invictus 7
The Prudence Crandall House in Canterbury,
    Connecticut 9
Las Percales 12
Sports 13
Green Animals 14
The House Party 16
Hittites 19
David 20
A Poem Beginning with a Line by Wyatt 21
The Painting 22
Fresh Horses Should Be Waiting 24
Grinders 26
Vicarious Animals 28
The Fat Baby 31
Nancy Drew 32
Daisy or Jane? 33
The Crybaby at the Library 37
Do You Traipse 39
Louie 40
About Calder 41
Herbert Smith 42
The Foamy-Necked Floater 43
Walden Remaindered 45
Sacagawea 46
The Phoenix 53

The House Party

I Have Met Freddy

I have met Freddy again in the masterful gazebo.
This time he brought along his collection of marble statues
   (tiny) and he brought Daphne
Peterson who is staying on another three weeks at the Lion,
   because the Nantucket people
have not gotten out of her house. The cutest—far and
   away—statue
is a shepherdess who is taking a thorn out of one of her
   charge's feet, Androcles-like,
and it is quite unornamented, unlike the others, which are
   tartishly polychromed.
Daphne was saying that terry cloth is a good bet for the—
   then we were interrupted by

birds! flinging themselves against the vines! madly trying to
   get into the gazebo.
Not understanding what was happening, we all three took
   fright, although pretending to be amused.
Daphne annoyingly fled into Freddy's arms, which were
   trying to fend off such birds as had penetrated the netting,
and while he was extremely flattered by Daphne's
   "advances," which really *were* advances,
he was also terribly peeved by having to do so many things
   at once.
Suddenly all the birds went away, off to bash into something
   else, and Daphne unwound her cashmere hands with
   silvery-pink *long* fingernails from around poor brave
   Freddy's neck,
and a few birds that were left clutched rather faintly at the
   inside netting, wanting out again, after all that.
Daphne and I picked up all the marble figures and wrapped
   them in their tissue paper and put them back in the box.

Freddy said that if he had been any kind of anything at all he would have brought one of those walking sticks that has brandy secretly inside, and you screw off the head and quaff with your friends, and then you suggest that everybody walk down to the outbuildings and look at the new baby pigs born last week, they are doing so well.

Rachel and Wally

That girl needing rescuing out there in the boat
—her friend is back hysterical on the shore—
the former the girlfriend of that boyfriend of each
of whom it was observed this morning when we saw them hitch
but picked them not up, on the way to our boring aunt's
place up in Portsmouth, New Hampshire: these kids these days!
at their nonsectarian coed day and boar-
ding school of rustic suburban rightish stance!
popping with rhetorical questions, afloat
in blancmange literally or sinking in it, says:
the wrong sestet hooked up with the right octave?
Would I swallow that, hook line and sinker? "Not wav-
ing but drowning" (Stevie Smith) and yet
remember the dryads are the ones that are always wet.

The Cavendish Club

I was fossicking in the bookstacks not long ago over a
   semantic and epistemological botherment
involving a latent appearance of the petrified dative, and
   ultimately languishing over it,
so I got Angela on the horn and I said Angela
get me the man from DARE, which is the Dictionary
of American Regional English. And I said CASSIDY?
but all I got was the operator and she was a man
and he was in the middle of arranging to have lunch with
   Angela.
Cassidy is the Man from DARE in Madison,
Wisconsin, who is remembered as the most recent
editor of Bright's Anglo-Saxon Grammar and Reader,
formulated originally by a favorite henchman and
   trencherman
of James A. H. Murray, the compiler of the OED,
who nearly died of pneumonia in his spongy workshop
and didn't, alas, live long enough to see publication
in 1908. Well, after Angela and I had screeched at each other
over the airwaves of the intercom, to the delight of
   everybody,
including Cassidy, whom Angela had finally gotten hold of
(but then we were cut off), I went off to lunch myself, as a
   matter of fact,
at the Cavendish Club, which is a great deal too expensive to
   belong to,
and was named after the gang of thugs which started the
   Lone Ranger on his lifetime of doing good,
the Cavendish gang. In the front hall there is a sofa
entirely upholstered in marabou and extremely tickly.
Anyway I was just putting away some of the curried broccoli
   bisque when I was brought the telephone

and it was Mrs. Farley crying AUGGH! I'm so *depressed*, so I
   lunged on over there.
Mrs. Farley lives at the moment in a reconverted Richardson
   railroad station
which she has caused to be moved to Irvington-upon-
   Hudson, so the lunging took a bit of time;
also she is exceedingly independent and does not have a
   maid but has her dogs answer the door,
a pair of Brittany spaniels who love visitors and would
   probably kiss any burglar to death.

Such IRONY, said Mrs. Farley, it is precisely about the
   Cavendish Club that I want to talk to you.
The problem is that they want to tear it down and make it
   into locker rooms for the Cathedral of St. John the Divine,
which is practically my favorite parish, second only I think
   to the one in Jackson Hole
where behind the altar there is just plate glass giving out on
   the Tetons, if that's what they are.
Yet I am aware that you are aware that the Cavendish, while
   masquerading as the stuffy retreat of those slightly to the
   right of McKinley,
actually teaches ex-convicts to cook very well, harbors
   meetings of feminists and minority groups and physically
   and mentally handicapped people,
and that it likewise lets various indigent artists live there
   almost for free, and everyone thinks they are
   stockbrokers,
so demolition would be ghastly. I couldn't get the bishop
but I got his very sensible suffragan, who said that the
   desserts at the Cavendish
are splendid and maybe we can work something out.
                                                      Being
   of one mind with Mrs. Farley,
I barked some long-distance orders at Angela, and then
   began to make a huge list

of everyone Mrs. Farley and I could think of who had
    anything to do with anything,
and we spent three days pestering them and then six weeks
    later we got terrific results,
which were that the Cathedral chapter would not tear down
    the Cavendish but would secretly use it for lots of their
    own programs,
and the Cavendish after a sandblasting would go on existing
    as it always had,
except that it had to be renamed the Fiona Birdsey Agape
    Foundation, in honor of the trustee who coughed up most
    of the muscle and wherewithal.

Thither Mrs. Farley and I recently repaired to toast our
    (partial) triumph, and she revealed to me that it had just
    been revealed to her by the Cavendish pastry cook
that he makes his brownies with the regular Betty Crocker
    family-size brownie mix
but for the ⅓ cup of water he substitutes ⅓ cup of Jim Beam
and that's why they're so delicious. Munching some
    agreeably betimes,
I contemplated Angela and a spiffy unknown at a window
    table, to whom I raised my chilly glass.

Sol Invictus

"Christ the true sun is risen in the dying of the day":
something those anonymous-Christian aborigines knew
   perfectly well
in the winter solstice, mixing up Easter with Christmas.

Various folk plays, waits and mummings persuade us
likewise of the virtue of portents, and the Bayeux Tapestry
   people,
Romanesque fellows—ISTI MIRANT STELLA, they marvel at
   the star

which in fact is a comet—with their egglike eyes.
But the song that went along with it all is sung and gone,
being oral-formulaic and sidereally "lost,"

unlettered; and then there's the problem of liturgy
vs. literature, because where does one leave off
and the other begin? and what about Baumstark's

Second Law, which says that the most important
parts of the ritual remain in their original languages?
Oh, the holy day is connected to the stones of cities

(where were *your* spiritual ancestors at the problematic
   parting of the *soi-disant* Red Sea?
arguing about pig bones in the wilderness of Lachish?
or painting themselves blue and worshiping fir trees?)

and to a monomythic talisman such as the relic,

except that you can't *have* a relic if there's a resurrection,
and you certainly can't have a horn from the ox

at Bethlehem, since the ox was a late fabrication
from an apocryphal gospel factory. Nor a tailfeather
of the Holy Ghost. The point is that the physical object

is thought to impart sacramental energy, a touchstone
in the material suffused with the divine, composed
of not so much Christmas or Easter, orgy and trauma,

as a safe and solemn passage to other places—here's where
    the monomyth comes in again—the bearer
is a shapeshifter in a curious chariot whose days are
    lengthening!

The Prudence Crandall House in Canterbury, Connecticut

The other day when we were driving back from the Yale
   Game on back roads "into blue obscurity,"
we went past the most divine house with the most incredible
   rooflines
and excellent cornices and quoins in Canterbury.
It's the Prudence Crandall house and she bought it in 1833
   for $2,000
and nobody knows when it was actually built but it was
   there in 1815,
and Miss Crandall started an academy in it which is to say
   the equivalent of a high school
at the behest of the Canterbury residents. Meanwhile,
   Prudence had a black servant
named Sarah Harris whose father was William Lloyd
   Garrison's
distributor for the *Liberator*, the abolitionist newspaper. Well,
   Sarah
asked to come to class, and naturally Prudence let her
and that was her big mistake, because the citizens objected,
reasonably as they thought, since they had hired Prudence
   for their white daughters.
So Prudence went off to Boston and had an exhaustive talk
   with said William Lloyd Garrison,
and *he* said she ought to open a boarding school in
   Canterbury
for black girls, and he gave her the names and addresses
of lots of free black families in New England who could
   afford it! Aha!
Prudence dismissed her white students and recruited black
   ones,
telling the enraged townspeople that she was going to teach
   whomever she wanted to.

The citizens, embattled for fair, held a lot of private meetings
    and then a Town Meeting, to wheedle Prudence out of it.
Prudence wouldn't budge, and the first black student
    arrived
on April 1. The citizens got up a petition which resulted in
    the passage
of the so-called Black Law and black is what it was
because it said that no person could cross the state line into
    Connecticut to be educated there if the people in the town
    where the education was going to take place didn't want
    them to (this idiotic act was fortunately repealed in 1838).
Anyway, back in June of 1833 Prudence was arrested for
    transgressing the Black Law,
spending the night in jail, which humiliated the citizens, for
    some reason, but not Prudence.
The newspapers, abolitionist and otherwise, had an absolute
    field day.
Three trials took place, the first was a hung jury, the second
    with a conviction
which was thrown out on a technicality, and the third
    acquitted her.
The abolitionist press was extremely disappointed when she
    got off
because they'd hoped to get a lot of mileage
out of appealing the case to the Supreme Court and really
    making a splash.
Well, the acquittal made the Canterbury residents, on the
    other hand, completely beside themselves,
and they threw stones through all of Prudence's beautiful
    windows and put manure down the well,
the students were excommunicated from the Congregational
    Church across the street,
and the doctor wouldn't treat them when they were sick.

But now while these indignities were going on and on,
    Prudence had gotten married

to a Baptist minister named Calvin Philleo
who convinced her no, it won't do, it won't work, give up
   the school. She sold the house,
they traveled: New York State, Illinois, she taught, they
   settled, gentlemen songsters,
finally, in Elk Falls, Kansas, of all places, where she lived till
   past the War
and well into Reconstruction. No children.

Las Percales (Smooth Percale Sheets?)

I am going down to Las Percales
which is admired for its clement atmosphere

A model of Stonehenge is there in spongecake monoliths
Seals flip and come to rest with happy thuds

I will not leave Las Percales for any tootle

Far over the fuzzy expanses lie the extremities (I honor
   them)
which have tiptoed me to the enclosure of cloudy beauty

Sports

Oh, don't you love sports and the dazzling thrill of contest!
as a result of which there are lovely cups and ribbons

like a silver statue of the Statue of Liberty holding
a tennis racket strung with silver chickenwire

which ought to be catgut (which is actually sheep's innards)
which once long ago I beheld on a bridesmaid's bookcase,

and was I deeply bothered as a kid that they
cut up cats to make tennis rackets. A natural

material, catgut, like the horsehide spheroid of mounds
across the nation, a substance more august

than the vile pigskin of football which Francine
du Plessix Gray so rightly calls "that disgusting

spectacle." But they don't use horse but cowhide in these
 latter days
in the majors, a sacred taboo that is straight out of Tacitus

where horses are holy beings. The number of stitches
in the baseball is regulated by law and they're all

made in Haiti. The pigmonger now of the November tube
is naugahyde. There's a lot of USDA *boeuf bourguignon*
 stalking around out there,

some bearing a palpable resemblance to bubblegums.
Figure to yourself these observations of simple spectators.

Green Animals

Miss Brayton clipped the boxwood
leaf by leaf herself
although she had
a gardener
for every tree

The boxwood grow
fantastically in the
architected shapes
the gardeners taught them
There every hedge
winds around a green
boxwood animal

llamas made of trees
a green rabbit
a bear with its arm around another bear

Miss Brayton called her house
Green Animals
It looks at Narragansett Bay
The boxwood garden
doesn't mind the salt
It flourished then
It flourishes now

Miss Brayton invited
Hope Slade from Providence
weekend after weekend
year after year

and when Hope was married
and dressing for her wedding

in the morning
Miss Brayton sent
her driver in her car
full of white flowers, full of them
all the way to Providence

so Hope's mother's house
was covered with white
vases and nosegays   bunches
urns of branches and flowerpots   bouquets
buckets of white arms of flowers
and there was no place to sit down

The House Party

We were invited to a house party last weekend in Lake
 Forest, Illinois, which I shall not soon
forget, and this is not only because I brought what turned
 out to not be the right clothes for it,
but, more objectively, the people were alarming at best.
When I got up in the middle of Friday night there were lots
 of the guests
running through the hall and leaping in and out of each
 other's rooms together,
who mercifully didn't see me. I had to call them all
by their first names except Mrs. Farley, even though I shall
 never see any of them again,
such as Davenport and Davis, Manfred, Ritzinda, Conall
 and Yvette.
I remarked to Davenport when we were playing croquet
 that my second son at the age of three had cleverly been
 wont
to refer to croquet mallets as golf hammers, at which
 Davenport laughed not at all;
yet, to be fair, realizing that he had been less than
 sympathetic, he very kindly told me
the plot of the Thorne Smith he had been reading the
 previous night, although I bet that's not all he was doing.
Davenport confided to me over several pousse-cafés that he
 is a grain arbitrator,
and then Manfred (one of the world's worst names) came
 along and we talked about grain.
Usually I like to talk to men but it was difficult to talk to
 these ones
or difficult for them to talk to me at any rate, but that was
 OK
because it transpired that the women talked together a great
 deal in little pockets.

Ritzinda true to *her* name wore a dress that had only one
shoulder and not much of that on Saturday for dinner.
Mrs. Farley told me I should put apricot oil on my face a
little at a time and it would be absolutely wonderful,
much the way Davenport had talked about grain, although I
certainly don't think Mrs. Farley was in the apricot oil
business.
Ritzinda of the single shoulder asked me who I'd gotten to
get me invited,
and looked somewhat addled when I said that a cousin of a
college classmate of Yvette's had been my brother's piano
teacher
and that some of these shared the same cleaning woman in
Georgetown,
which is all perfectly true, if boring. Mrs. Farley
may possibly be a hundred and goes around completely
covered with Liberty scarves,
and as one might expect there was dancing Saturday night
well into Sunday
at which she excelled, scarves and all, and it turned out she
had known the violinist as a young man.
Some of the other things we talked about were Carl Rogers,
shallots, bargello,
tobacco barns, curare, giving people *la question* during the
French Revolution and after,
encaustics of the tobacco barns, which are Yvette's idea of
lares et penates,
David Riesman, James Agee, and exchange students in the
Philippines.
Mason, to whom I am married and whose job is teaching
church law to seminarians for a living and with whom I
went to this house party,
and who incidentally got the better of the deal, can't figure
out why I'm being so disagreeable,
inasmuch as *he* spent the whole weekend in the study with a
marvelous and very complete collection of church law
books

dating back incredibly far in their original bindings, and
    reading practically all of them,
and showing up for meals and cocktails during which he
    explained to Emery and Rosfrith Van de Sand
the complete history of church law, which if they had been
    going to seminary would have cost them
hundreds and hundreds of dollars, and they didn't even
    have to buy the texts,
although the Van de Sands probably couldn't have gotten
    admitted to seminary anyway
even if they'd wanted to; but of that they will doubtless
    remain forever unaware.

Hittites

Hittites rode by on contemporary village machines
I don't speak Hittite; Christine does, but she wasn't there

Yaz the Distinguished acknowledged
the puffing of the populace
a Nubian held aloft his plate of kippers

Your eyes will be the eyes of the basilisk, my lamb
when you behold how I left the rice
boil over while I watched them go by

Next Saturday is Hittite Saturday!
As far away as Ravenna, people will be in touch with their
    feelings!

David

David rode sensibly over the asphalt reticulations,
his breath as sweet as apples.

"Back from Topeka in your *baba-au-rhum* boots!
Was it boring? The Dervishes are here."

"Fish is inexpensive for a lot of people,
chowder smooth and easy and gives a Provençal tone."

"I love a harpsichord David but I love you more.
Wendy looks as though she might faint."

"We have not perspired so much from the heat.
It is rustic here, lovely and lonely as the president of Henri
    Bendel."

"Meantime you cheerfully proceed stateside to an extreme
    tower
covered with battens and bring me a Mickey Finn."

So soon as she held his arm, she kept from crying.
Then, freckled and muscled, his arm was—oof—fast round
    her in the dark and they heard
the ghastly syndics reciting the Thirty-Nine Articles.

A Poem Beginning with a Line by Wyatt

They flee from me that sometime did me seek
at 2:30 A.M. in the morning tiptoeing around considerately
so as not to wake people up
not that I care about it particularly any more
or about the notion of the rejection experience
on the theoretical level. Something is wrong
with a relationship anyway in which a participant
evinces no hostility toward another participant?

There was one thing I remember over and over
Dear love how like you this or rather
how do I like it myself since you won't get a look
Fine but there could be a lot better timing
and the juxtapositions make me edgy so that I
start talking to myself but I'm writing it all down
in dramatic form like several monologues
or role-playing is what it's valuable as probably

The Painting

My mother will put it in a poem, for God's sake, of which
   Uncle Nick will do a woodcarving.
And then Trintje will take a photograph of it which she will
   kodalith.
My father will write a law about the kodalith, and then his
   father-in-law, my Grandpa Tom
will say why it makes a better statute than an ordinance.
Then Aunt Sarah who is married to Uncle Nick will put it in
   one of her hairy weavings and will also make a Library of
   Congress catalogue card for it,
and Aunt Betsy will find out if it is sick, and if it has a
   temperature she will give it an antibiotic but not if it does
   not (Aunt Betsy is medically conservative, which my
   mother appreciates).
Uncle Tom who is married to Aunt Betsy and is personnel
   director of a huge factory in Bristol, Rhode Island,
will put it in a box marked THISSIDEUP and read a paper about
   it at a plastics convention.
Aunt Sarah and Uncle Nick have a baby named Hopey and
   she will put it in her mouth.
Uncle Tom and Aunt Betsy have two little kids named
   Wisner and Laura who stand up in rowboats.
(Laura is really Laura Ingalls Jansen and is a genuine cousin
   of *Little House on the Prairie* on the Ingalls side.)
They find us bratty sometimes but everyone is bratty
   sometimes.
Granny Hope who is married to Grandpa Tom will make a
   watercolor of all of us when we are doing the above at a
   cookout,
and it will be like that picture in the Museum of Fine Arts
   called something like "The Children of Mr. and Mrs. van

Rensselaer Satterthwaite" where the children are sitting around the living room next to vases and sofas reading books and doing other things that they like.

Fresh Horses Should Be Waiting

The lady and   Fresh horses should be waiting
Julia try to help   for the tired riders and there should be oats
with the horses   and blankets, Julia,
                 for the sweating ones they leave; we must
                    walk them
                 up and down and up and down—Oh God,
                 that's the boring part of horses, not the
                    manure.

An observation   Get the men a large kettle of water with
period   dipper and ice;
                 their rugs and robes spread out very well on
                    the ground.
                 Get them tiny brandy glasses with gold fruit
                    pictured on them. Get them brandy.
                 We can lie down along the fringes now that
                    it is dark
                 and stroke the backs of their arms while we
                    listen to them sing.

The centuries   Children who sit quietly like us and read to
revisit them   you aloud
unbidden   remind us of our puritan forebears or who
                    we would have been then
                 if we had sat thus by what Stevenson called
                    "the cold candle"
                 and uttered little alphabets, a New England
                    primitive in your own home.
                 It was peculiar that they had to wear hats in
                    the house.

They look for Dear Julia, you have always been such a
the resolution   comfort to me,
 walking unembarrassed on every quadrant
     of the map.

Grinders

Certain parties in Beantown call them submarines
and Philadelphia lawyers sometimes call them hoagies,
but the Portuguese kind of grinders, which can be found in
   the bailiwick

of Narragansett Bay as you look at the U.S. Coast
and Geodetic Survey Chart are the best, containing
not your ordinary roofing-type lettuce, but pulverized
   cabbage;

yet they're also called submarines in Chicago (or, more
   austerely,
subs), which makes no sense at all. (You can get in a similar
   pickle
with soda pop, which in sections of, say, New Bedford,

Fall River or Mattapoisett is called tonic,
to the confusion of [gin-drinking] hairdressers from
   elsewhere.)
Grinders be the world's primordial comestible:

slices of A, B and C surrounded by D
and elmered together with olive oil, pepper and oregano
as designed in the dawn of time and coinciding

with the invention of Primitive Art by the First Adam
with a growly stomach under his version of the Charter Oak,
so symbolic and meaningful and so forth, on account of how
   the bread

has got all the associations of bread, no? and a salami
symbolizes phallic symbols, quadrupeds, and auguring the
   future by entrails.

The lettuce or cabbage or what have you means new green
   life,

although that's pretty sappy and obvious. It's abotulistic,
   and it also symbolizes,
and indeed contains, chlorophyll, which symbolizes in turn
the absence of halitosis, a consummation

devoutly to be you-know-what. Oh, you might say the Four
   Basic Food groups ride here together at anchor in your
   grinders
like Righteousness and Peace kissing each other in Psalm
   Eighty-Five.

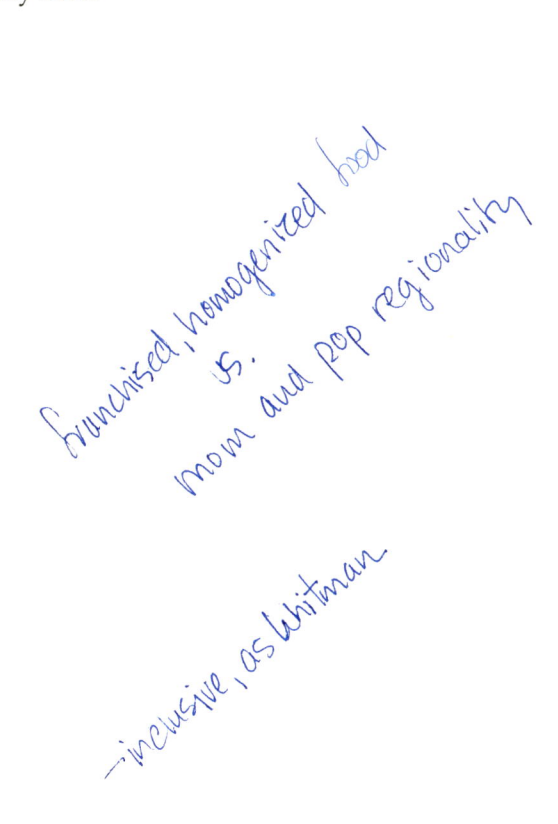

franchised, homogenized food vs. mom and pop regionality

—inclusive, as Whitman

27

Vicarious Animals

The mustering vertebrates (and some invertebrates too,
 necessarily)
are looking so *forward* to the hunt, most of them, with
 friendly persistence;
these six months have been devoted to garnering munitions
 and waybread—
harquebuses and fowling-pieces, hoof polish, klaxons,
Pepperidge Farm and Catherine Clark heels, a complicated
 suet *pâté* for fifty ("Upton Sinclair Surprise"),
buffalo rugs, calves-foot jelly, ginger beer.
The Three Kittycats Gruff (one of them a Mackerelsnatcher
 and two Anglo-Catholics)
and the fenduck from the outback asseverate drooly oaths,
assuring themselves and each other that they are competent
 and valiant
which is privately doubted by an ancient matted spaniel,
an expert in Appalachian and European (Hummel-type) clog
 dancing,
sporting a Stassen button, carrying an epergne full of
 macadamia nuts,
and clutching a nasty cheap paper edition of the I-Can-Read
 Gilgamesh,
which will entertain his nephew in the campaign dusk.
So no more rusticating (*rus in rure*) or hibernating,
 estivating, or any of that stuff
for dear Puffkin and Muffkin (old spelling: Poughkyn and
 Moughkyn).
Tabby and Bowser are wrested from the arms of Morpheus,
 Bossy from cropping the delicate legumes.
Now for propitiation in the fanes, now trying out the wedge-
 shaped formations,

squeezing selves into old uniforms, sighing over the greater
   girths,
come Reynard and Chanticleer, Partlet and other obvious
   notorious and showoffy glittery literary types:
Old Yeller, the Red Pony, White Fang, Sounder, Grendel, the
   Empress of Blandings.
Monsters, of course, are included, not least for purposes of
   allegory,
and this brings up a difficulty: interanimal relationships
en route. A problem for sure is the Conan Doyle outfit,
The Hound of the Baskervilles, the Giant Rat of Sumatra for
   which the world is not yet prepared,
Silver Blaze and the Speckled Band and others, nobody's
   sweet domestic critters.
The situation is complicated by a bunch of eminent animal
   consultants,
Marguerite Henry, Joy Adamson of blessed memory, James
   Herriot, Marianne Moore,
Captain Kangaroo USN (Ret.), Albert Payson Terhune, both
   Walts, St. Francis, Swift, and Aesop.
(Quantities of potential candidates were considered and
   rejected
and have spent a lot of time being offended [yet are secretly
   relieved,
because of the hunt's onerous, arduous nature, and because
   sometimes the animals are tedious]).
The consultants encourage them with "Hold your horses,
   my fine feathered friend! Lord love a duck!
Take a gander at that Newfoundland!" which the animals get
   pretty tired of.
Music is important, together with reading aloud,
and it gets the animals through such a lot of bad moments.
   Especially madrigals,
such as "To Spot upon Going to the Wars," "To Spot upon
   Being Afraid of Going to the Wars,"

ballads ("I've Been Working on the Whale-Road"), an
unbelievable amount of tacky barbershop, motets, Moody
and Sanky,
and a little cantata for sweet potato and flageolet: "To Spot
upon—OH BOY—Not Having to Go to the Wars after All."

Yet despite this frenetic support they ambivalently
procrastinate by going to the theater, opera and movies
—oh, they go to "Equus," "The Night of the Iguana," "Cat
on a Hot Tin Roof," "The Frogs," "101 Dalmatians," "Porgy
and Bess"—
and make up inspiring mottoes and copy them down:
Domimina Nustio illumea (and a lot of good that one does)
and coats of arms to go with,
and they argue at the last minute about routes and passes
and riparian rights that haven't obtained in years;
but there's no help for it! they all cry in their indigenous
God-given noises,
some in fairly decent iambic pentameter
or jolly old dactyls with plenty of "free" free verse sprinkled
in between, and almost no end rhyme,
everybody acting foul, acting like silly geese, like studs, like
turkeys,
acting sheepish, foxy, horny, owlish, batty, dogged, and
humping,
acting wise as doves and harmless as serpents, acting
pusillanimous,
acting catty, doing the bunny hop, acting pig-headed, hot
dogging, chickening out,
eating crow, acting drunk as a skunk, mad as a wet hen, off
they go now.

The Fat Baby

the fat baby is in her own thought
she is rocked on her self
she is her basket

her fingers make a star for themselves
around anything

a rabbit is inside her   or is that milk
if milk   how fuzzy

> *Handwritten annotations:*
> we are the center of our world
>
> warm, fuzzy, comforting, protected
>
> self-containment
> babies have the power to command;
> little self-contained worlds
> —a "one-year surreal moment"—
> a nameless, unnamed moment
> at its best

Nancy Drew

Tripping over road apples, we entered the bone orchard for
   a necktie party,
duded up in ratcatchers and loaded to the Plimsoll line
   with stool pigeons, polecats, sidewinders, and firewater.
The Smith and Wesson (property of the Nation's Attic)
   provided a leaden Powder River (of the National Pastime)
   past the trembling cannon-fodder,
sitting ducks who took a powder in fuzzmobiles to keep
   their powder dry,
hard by wall-to-wall stiffs, poison pens, the numbers game,
   and other war horses and old chestnuts.
Well, the upshot was a rhubarb, a donnybrook, a Chinese
   fire drill:
gumshoe Roman Policier, eschewing mentor's coke and
   Strad, clapped the bracelets
on Manuel Laboro of uncertain address, and subsequently
   "twitch't his Mantle blue" and amscrayed,
brandishing his bumbershoot and flicking his tufera into the
   cuspidor.

Daisy or Jane?

The reason the rug is matted
is that the dog always lay there
rug upon rug you might say
warm and flat and warm and flat

We have two dictionaries
Big Fat and American H.
I Xeroxed the sweet educational
puffin picture in the latter

Come! we will have good sandwiches and lemonade
They make this very well here
We love the moonlight and animals
and you see we do not like discomfort

Daisy has grown weary while "stirring our porridge"
She receives letters from everybody
All are covered with a tempo of glitter
tears, pumpkin seeds, feet and their grains of sand

Daisy helps with the animals still
It is keen of her to do it
She is trying to finish *Swann's Way*
and is partly through the second volume

* * * *

I walk with her often in the "mental kibbutz." Daisy doesn't sleep well. Her last job was with Mrs. Farley of blessed memory. Mrs. Farley was like a cellist, a snood, a beautiful child beset by math. Daisy was her companion I don't know how many years.

There is a new and happy person, said Daisy, called
Adamant Raisin. That is a pretty disgusting name, I said.
You are always unkind! We will go to table now. Critick
Marie has poured water. Water of life!

Critick Marie figures but little here
She is immensely pretty and startles joy
She can pour a mean glass of water
bugle beads cantaloupe   bacon rind   Smithers

But this is all so *fragwürdig*
Adamant Raisin turns out to be great
and I regret my horridness
We will become close

* * * *

You didn't tell me that Adamant Raisin was a young
Byronic man. Well, no, *vous avez raisin*! It is like Freddy all
over again without the weak chin. No, it is not like Freddy.
It is like: 2 cups of Quaker oatmeal, 1 cup brown sugar
firmly packed, 3 eggs, a cup of—rub into scalp thoroughly.
Now you're horrid again! Just horrid! your ambivalence is
your best attribute and I don't see much of that! This is
absolutely true, truer by far than myth or motif, which
languish!

So heave to, my snuggies, it is time for a sacramental.
How do we know? Let's talk about people now. Daphne P.
has been married six times—once to a plant. I Daphne P.
take thee Circassian Rubber Tree to my wedded husband.
Well, if he's a rubber tree, that's why there's no issue, right?
heh heh. Horrid again and this time to poor Daphne P. who
probably never had a chance. What were her other ones

like? Don't you suppose defect of form? What's for chow?
Chickiform emporkments. They have stock in the Piggies'
Farm.

    Adamant Raisin delivered himself of a poem at dinner. It
was a very quiet night and a poem about his ancestors
coming to this country, from Holland. It was about guilt.
Adamant Raisin had discovered that his family (the
Hardenburghs) had been the oppressors (in upstate New
York) of SOJOURNER TRUTH! childhood idol of all. Adamant
Raisin felt very bad about this and prayed that the poem
expiate the vileness of his progenitors. Daisy, why did you
not give me an inkling of such depths?

Eheu brothers of the lime-ring, pollen spelunk

was the beginning of the next poem. It was about ducks and
dessert came at once, floating in ethereal little glass bowls.
They were from Murano. Then we went and had spiced tea
and did crafts with expired credit cards and olives.
Everyone was from Murano.

* * * *

Jane was painting a picture
of each salamander as it crawled out of the drain
thinking of the constitution of Costa Rica

"You shouldn't name someone Victor
What if he turned out to be a loser?
But Victoria is pretty—can't explain"

Whit sat gladly on the wall
He was in love with Jane

The late blue light of an early frost
partly obscured her visibility

"Dear Jane: You are the hammock of my past
bearing the harvest of next year, the melon of ocean
When you lay your brush like a muffin
in the pigment of the smelting of fractiousness
dust flees before it sees you coming
Macadam lays itself bright at your toes
Windsor no more the apartheid of Newton
dear Jane you are my oxymoron"

"Whit," said Jane, "you're a civil servant
tell me about the strikes in the Trenton factory"
They drove through the night in Whit's brown car
brave into the full dawn to brunch at The Lion

A note is pinned to Jane's banana napkin
It is written in a fist that is very much like Daisy's

"All suspiring, Prince, is a conflation
of *Pericles* and *As You Like It*
I mostly bomb socially
even if I think I am Apollonius of Tyre
even although I should be Apollinaire heading south on a
    bike
even if I am a Barbara Guest Lecturer
even when I tell the Union Oyster House joke"

The Crybaby at the Library

There was a crybaby at the library.
Tears were pouring heavily down his face.
He had omitted to do his math
and thought of the anger of his teacher
as the tears fell on his knitted
mittens between the fingers and thumb.

It is raining all over inside the library.
Parts of the brick walls are curling up
and plaster is falling on the heads and beards of students.
It is very dangerous for the books.
The rain comes down from every beam
and the professors do not know whether they should wrap
their articles in themselves or themselves in their articles.
The beautiful new botany professor who is only twenty-six
    and has marvelous dark eyes
has makeup running down her face as she runs out the door.

A precious incunabulum inside a glass case
is swimming gently as if in a dishpan.
Tiny letters and pieces of gold that were put there in 1426
are lifting off and turning into scum.
The assistant librarians are afraid to use the telephones
because yellow sparks are coming out of them.
Several young men go up to the attic, saying that the trouble
    may be from up there.
The electricity goes off and people are standing
between the floors in dangerously wet elevators.
The librarians' Kleenex and aspirin are wet and are melting
    into each other in the desk drawers.
The Shakespeare professors come out of the Shakespeare
    Room

and look around and go back in again; they must stay with
   the ship.
Fog is rising like rugs between the bookstacks.
People are laughing in a brittle way to disguise their well-
   grounded panic.

The botany professor is a redemptive figure.
She goes to the Maintenance Department and reports what
   is happening in the library.
Eventually the Maintenance Department goes over and fixes
   things.
The crybaby is definitely *not* a redemptive figure—he sits
still self-absorbed and shivery, and crying and crying,
and not at all trying to catch up on his math, nor even trying
   to fake it,
and all the time waves of water dash over his Bean boots
and up onto his lap, splashing his notebooks.
For the impending disgust of his teacher is foremost in his
   mind
as tears are foremost on his cheeks, where he sits crying and
   crying in the library.

Do You Traipse

Do you traipse long-leggedly through murky woodlands?
you are such an Abercrombie-looking person
especially today in various grays and duns
and I am always taken aback by stuff like that

This is not to say that I'm not your hearty
supporter because I am. I am just sort of
mystified, your mystique mystifies me
and I wish that when you were dishing out

municipal admonishments and info to the great unwashed
which is always your honor of course that
you were sending some neat special message
designed for me alone and for me perennially

but you obviously aren't and it's very much better
as it is than as above which is all too goony.
These are occasions to pretend to overlook
and turn the gaze to new constructs, perhaps in the snow,
    and squint dispassionately at their elevations.

Louie

You told me I would be your
light star and I said aha
that's bright   that's great

Meet me where the lights
of the World's Fair never
go out   We are the

Elgin Marbles   We are
the Crystal Palace of 18-aught
54   We are the cow

at the Springfield Exposition
balancing a peck of
cucumbers on her back

    No other cow could
    but we see us do it

About Calder

In my own view friction fittings are small monuments
even though you say they aren't practical like a threading
I love them and I love cogs too on bikes
Whoever invented them I'd like to shake his hand

A painter stays at our house—he is painting our children—
and in the mornings it takes him ages to make himself
    scrambled eggs
whipping and folding them as if they were colors
But then finally he is saying: Zee sobway ees feeneesh!

I am writing to you about Calder
his metallurgy   his space minerals
Once when it was way below zero my hand stuck to one of
    the discs
—risky, inductive and prime, and also scattered, I remember

Herbert Smith

Aha! how would it be to walk into a crowded church and
   shout,
     "Your psalms are all derivative! and gratuitous!"
and then run out again and hide among the people and
   pretend to be at prayer
        Such penitents,
         panting like little animals,
are charmers, waiters and candle-makers, changers of the
   raw dish and diaper.

I myself can taste the apocalyptic
as you can, though my perception of it is different.
       You have taken five
       apples, four apples
out of the basket, and Herbert Smith will put three in.

Herbert Smith represents Everyman in this poem.
Numbers are not important to the quality of the
   abovementioned child and grown ups.
       Not in church,
       not in chapel,
he is not a rock singer, he is not a stone-thrower, he is
   content in the first light.

The Foamy-Necked Floater

Here come the crazy professors with their complicated recording machines and other equipment.
Look you, Vlasci, the one has the spectacles of iron.
Do they want our daughters, the black-eyed ones?
No, little Rugosa will fold her shawl twice, whistling the while.
So Professor Grundtwig came once, to the land of our remote cousins, across the French flood.
Many hazards awaited him eponymously in the mountains of stone, stark and barren, giants' work,
and he brought with him an inestimably enriching cultural background,
whereof he likewise received much himself in return, and then he went away again at last.
So also the singer Jorge Luis Borges sings of our singing (who is not to be confused with Isaac Bashevis Singer),
and he has not even been here, by Allah, except in a kind of spirituo-literary sense.

The professors entered the coffeehouses where we sing our songs with much politeness.
We glory in making them feel comfortable and at home, because Artü has a radio that gets baseball games from Washington, D.C.
Professor Caithness ap Caithness said with a flourish that all should receive zlotys;
it was not without pleasure that the townspeople accepted this information, throwing their little caps toward the earth-roof.
Do you know what a shock it is to eat grapes in the dark and get a rotten one that tastes like a cross between wine and dust?

43

If so, then you will have perceived of our joys and conflicts.
Phenolphthalein makes a fine impromptu ink, if you want to get any of this down.
Lo! what is it that flies now out of the sky? is it the falcon? is it the airplane? the rebuilt DC-10? oh, no, it is the falcon!
Dear God, what more is there to say? why should I lengthen my tale?

Walden Remaindered

This is the last cowboy song, this is the idiopathic font.
Myth meets behaviorism here and each finds the other
  frankly tacky.
There is a wall where you write sayings of Ben Franklin.
We seem to be coming to a consensus about this place; it is
  the enormous collar of which we are the collar buttons.
Wouldn't it be great to be renowned for your sayings?
As I have just said, there is a wall where you write sayings
  of Ben Franklin.
Afterward gray gulls feed those who want food from pewter
  objects (can you tell gull from object?—ask your friends).

The Past Municipal Pomegranate wears a blue velvet pillow
  on his head.
Two Kenneth Clarks? *Two* John Gardners?
Did you happen to notice Freddy, when Anita got the
  Walsingham Prize, how he looked right through her, as
  Cabbageface shook her hand, "alone and palely
  loitering"?
The epiphany of the protonutkin is always a daring dab.
And you are a teeming if proprietal hallelujah, an essay of
  ligaments of onion.
Here are a dozen Belgian handkerchieves (I do not know
  that that is the correct plural).
Look at Dürer's nifty logo; a monogram reduces one to an
  elixir.

her poems are conversational and like letters (epistolary) – a letter involves a mixture of styles, and information (informative). – a natural outflowing

Sacagawea

a letter is a written conversation.

No, Brown Claw, I do not wish to cut up the feet of the owl. I do not wish to boil them with sassafras root and wild garlic to make a broth for the Indian ague, and as a preventative of evil moods. I do not wish to hang the herbs to dry. Nor to render the tough skin of the buffalo for moccasin leather.

(old indian)

At least, I do not wish to do these things fourteen hours a day, although it is clear to me that I would be a/rat not to take my share of the boring work. For it is totally boring! For I wish to spend my days climbing mountains and learning about the wilderness. Goodbye, Brown Claw, I will stay no longer!

— change in tone

(colloquial)

* * * *

TOUSSAINT CHARBONNEAU:	*Eh bien*, I will tell you how you can get to the Pacific, M. Clark. My wife can take you. She's a Shoshone.
WILLIAM CLARK:	Your—HAW *(ha!)*—wife?
TOUSSAINT CHARBONNEAU:	*Ç'est ça.* Her experience of the Territory, the Divide, the Shoshone Country, *ç'est magnifique.*
WILLIAM CLARK:	Well, I don't know.
TOUSSAINT CHARBONNEAU:	Gentlemen, may I present my wife? Sacagawea, M. Lewis and M. Clark.
SACAGAWEA:	How do you do.

TOUSSAINT CHARBONNEAU: Dear love, we will be parted for a long time. It is only through you that these just men can achieve their final goal. I will watch and pray and trap furs. When you return from the Pacific, across the Rocky Mountains, you will find me waiting for you.

SACAGAWEA: Goodbye, dear love.

* * * *

It is funny to look at us. I would get up and look if I weren't so hungry. There are M. Lewis and M. Clark at head and foot being mother and father (don't know which is which). There is Cruzatte the voyageur licking his fingers; his French is very bad, unlike my sweetheart's; it is very messy nasal French. But he is kindness itself and a mad and beautiful dancer. The others are good men I believe. York especially is interesting sitting in the shadows being very very black.

* * * *

Mon cher Toussaint,

Nous avons voyagé pendant huit jours sans voir personne. Je suis bien triste quand je pense à toi. J'espère que M. de Champignon a acheté tous tes peaux. Est-ce que ses huskies sont revenu avec lui? Les oreilles des huskies étaient charmants. Je te quitte mon cher. Que le bon dieu te benisse toujours. *I leave you my dear. How to good old huskies return should bless you always.*

[Handwritten annotations: "We have traveled 8 days without seeing anyone. I'm sad when I think of you. I hope m. deC. has bought all your ? Did his ? with him?" and "skins" above "peaux"]

Sacagawea Charbonneau

M. Meriwether Lewis est drôle de type. Quand il fait *est a funny type   When he*

<u>had bad times he always sings funny american songs.</u>
mauvais temps il chante toujours les chansons américaines
assez amusantes.

* * * *

What Sacagawea wanted was a bath. She went down far
from the camp to a dark sidepool in the river and stretched
out in the shallows for a rest such as she had not had in
weeks. She washed her hair and scrubbed herself all over
with sand and leaves. Then she fell asleep in the sun with
the wind blowing around her, and slept and slept.

* * * *

The Song of Sacagawea

My mattress ticking is the pine;
the sleeping rabbit is my pillow.
I am traveling with M. Lewis and M. Clark.
They have asked me to guide them over the Rocky
    Mountains
and—*allez-houp*—back again.

They are doing a survey for the American Government.
We are going through many dangers,
we have voyaged across mountains and waters.
Always we meet amazing adventures;
I will mention some of the important ones.

Soon we will be coming to the Great Divide.
M. Clark who talks all the time
is going to find himself out of breath, in more ways than
    one.
√ M. Lewis talks into his journal, which will be valuable
    someday
to those who come after him, to learn about the country.

48

At first I was not willing to trust them
because of the Myth of the Performing Blossom Sticks
and in spite of Toussaint's good wishes.
But gradually I have come to believe they are good, I believe
  they are good!
While they were not paying attention, I have been observing
that they are quite honest in all their dealings,
e.g., they are kind and honorable to the Indians we meet on
  the trail.
Everyone in the party gets enough to eat, and nobody has to
  do more than a fair share of the chores.
There is a black servant in the party named York.
It would not be too much to say that the white men prefer
  his company to their own.
This is doubtless on account of his kind heart and his ability
  to tell jokes.
I will have a conversation with him by and by
on the subject of different races and colors and nationalities.
Now I must go and put bear grease on my parflèche.

* * * *

Mon cher Toussaint,
  Great Fir Cone a été ici hier soir mais nous ne l'avons pas
vu. Les scouts ont parlé avec lui dans le gulch. J'entends
que Great Fir Cone et ses guerrières doivent émigrer à
Wyoming. Il y a beaucoup d'hostilité entre les peuples.
                                                            ta S.
Enfin M. Clark a trouvé son Phillips head screwdriver.

* * * *

Cruzatte Tells the Legend of the Fire Monkeys

  Sacagawea and the leaders were resting in a mountain
cave out of the rain. Others in the party had gone for game.

49

The rain had continued many days. a fire dried their clothes and gear.

"I was on the Missouri," said Crusatte, "with a bunch of Menominee scouts and a party of Shoshone inimical to the Menominee. I figured I had them all over a barrel though because they couldn't move without my boat in the flood season. We had taken shelter in a river hut.

"The Menominee," went on Cruzatte, "could not eat the flesh of any animal that had been killed in the night. This, they explained, was because of a tribal dictum. The Shoshone said that they could not eat anything in the company of warriors who could not eat the flesh of an animal killed at night. I got out my dried food and some coffee and ate a little bit by myself. The Menominee said that they had to sing all during the daylight hours in the flood season. I wished that they had not had this rule, for the singing was tedious. The Shoshone leader said to me that he thought they didn't have any such rule but just wanted to be difficult. At nightfall the rain let up a little. I went outside.

"The Menominee party followed me presently. They gathered branches into a mound and as the moon slowly rose they began to stick feathers into the leaves. The Shoshone followed and gathered around them, and stood with their hands and toes pointing inward. Then they too began to put feathers into the pile of leaves. They stood around the mound in the moonlight, Menominee next to Shoshone, and in the sudden brightness I perceived that it was perhaps I that was the quarreler, the outsider."

* * * *

Toussaint,

This time I write in my own tongue, not in your lovely language, because I have not a good enough command of it

to tell you all that has transpired. I have been through such
perils as your St. Paul describes, and I compare myself,
though not very favorably, with your St. Joan. I lack
however their great faith to sustain me. I am alive
nonetheless through the providence of *le bon dieu*.
Meriwether and William are alive. But we are all battered,
from privation and sickness and fighting. The chief whom
we trusted so lately has now been revealed as a scoundrel
and horse thief. Our party has separated twice, despite the
good advice of Old Toby.
 I believe I will not tell you about the hunger and cold.
When we first saw the Pacific, it was a wonder and a beauty
and a terror. Now we are tired of it and long to be with
friends again. All the men tire of adventure. They are
talking about their sweethearts and I must as always forbear
to cry. Every day they used to write and write in their
books. Now they do not. I still think they are foolish who
have not learned to swim. In summer dear heart I will be
with you.

Your S.

* * * *

You couldn't get back over
back again like you want very well
and like the deal as set up
in those randy buckskin holey
boots and you didn't put
enough bear grease on them like I told you
enough times I am sorry to scold
I am from a matriarchal society remember
and sometimes this gets in the way of my independence
and respect for the feelings of other

Other than that I think we'll
get back OK and I must say

you are the good kind of explorers
I don't know what your government will do about this piece
   of woods
if anything but I'd like you to know
it has been a beautiful journey
I have enjoyed traveling with you very much

The Phoenix

At her swan song the phoenix bird whoopees
nodding to the Nordic pals in whom she delights
but for her basically give her anyday
the splendor of the east, her purples, the peacock blues,
mystical dots, horizontal suns, and what have you,
somewhat vulgar pyrotechnics which are a specialty

of nature at times; but none more sensational than the
    phoenix's
combustion! bother! what a pother! and a plethora
of wingy ashes after her bugling and fuguing
in funny junco and pigeon colors, every 900 or so years.

Just between you and me she rather
tends to overdo the symbolism aspect,
in an attempt to upstage the various heavies,
the pelican, owl and eagle, the *meaningful* dove.
Condescends to more boring birds like the turkey buzzard
who is intellectually gross and emotionally and esthetically
    ratty,
dismissed with whooshes of Essence de Rara Avis
from the atomizer, behind each ear as it were.

She sings, because she's fond of country music,
the beautiful nasal epimorph Roy Acuff wrote
exclusively for her. She is the Sole Arabian Bird
in her particular twilight of the gods
and gives us the Subtle Wink going under, peeping,
    scratching,
that's all folks, it all begins all over and
over again right now she knows we know she knows.

Other Titles in the Contemporary Poetry Series

James Applewhite, *Statues of the Grass*
Susan Astor, *Dame*
Hayden Carruth, *The Bloomingdale Papers*
Tony Connor, *New and Selected Poems*
Franz Douskey, *Rowing Across the Dark*
John Engels, *Vivaldi in Early Fall*
John Engels, *Weather-Fear: New and Selected Poems, 1958–1982*
Brendan Galvin, *Atlantic Flyway*
Brendan Galvin, *Winter Oysters*
Michael Heffernan, *The Cry of Oliver Hardy*
Philip Legler, *The Intruder*
Gary Margolis, *The Day We Still Stand Here*
Marion Montgomery, *The Gull and Other Georgia Scenes*
John Ower, *Legendary Acts*
Michael Pettit, *American Light*
Bin Ramke, *White Monkeys*
Paul Ramsey, *No Running on the Boardwalk*
J. W. Rivers, *Proud and on My Feet*
Vern Rutsala, *The Journey Begins*
Laurie Sheck, *Amaranth*
Myra Sklarew, *The Science of Goodbyes*
Paul Smyth, *Conversions*
Marcia Southwick, *The Night Won't Save Anyone*
Barry Spacks, *Imagining a Unicorn*
Mary Swander, *Succession*